DO YOU WANT A CAREER IN CRIMINAL JUSTICE?

JOBS IN THE COURT SYSTEM

KATHLEEN A. KLATTE

NEW YORK

Published in 2022 by The Rosen Publishing Group, Inc.
29 East 21st Street, New York, NY 10010

First Edition

Portions of this work were originally authored by Tamra B. Orr and published as *Careers in the Court System*. All new material in this edition was authored by Kathleen A. Klatte.

Library of Congress Cataloging-in-Publication Data

Names: Klatte, Kathleen A., author.
Title: Jobs in the court system / Kathleen A. Klatte.
Description: New York : Rosen Publishing, 2022. | Series: Do you want a career in criminal justice? | Includes index.
Identifiers: LCCN 2021010867 | ISBN 9781499470116 (library binding) | ISBN 9781499470109 (paperback) | ISBN 9781499470123 (ebook)
Subjects: LCSH: Courts--Vocational guidance--United States--Juvenile literature. | Law--Vocational guidance--United States--Juvenile literature. | Criminal justice, Administration of--Vocational guidance--United States--Juvenile literature. | Criminal justice personnel--United States--Juvenile literature. | Courts--United States--Automation--Juvenile literature. | Job vacancies--United States--Juvenile literature.
Classification: LCC KF297 .K53 2022 | DDC 347.73/1023--dc23
LC record available at https://lccn.loc.gov/2021010867

Manufactured in the United States of America

CPSIA Compliance Information: Batch #CSRYA22. For further information contact Rosen Publishing, New York, New York at 1-800-237-9932.

CONTENTS

INTRODUCTION

If you ask someone to name the biggest news stories of 1976, most would probably say the Bicentennial or the presidential election. However, people who lived in the vicinity of New York City might have a more sinister answer. For just over a year, local news was filled with reports of the serial murderer who signed himself "Son of Sam" on letters.

In August 1977, months of meticulous police work finally resulted in the arrest of David Berkowitz. An eyewitness reported seeing a man drive away from the scene of his final shooting in a car with a parking ticket on it. Very few tickets had been issued in the area that day and the police narrowed the search to Berkowitz, a postal worker who lived in Yonkers, NY.

The court system began processing evidence provided by police. This included bullets from the crime scenes, the "Son of Sam" letters, and Berkowitz's diaries. When questioned by police, Berkowitz explained that he'd been following the instructions of a demon who lived inside his neighbor's dog. Clearly, this was a very disturbed individual.

Initially, most people were surprised. Berkowitz looked very ordinary—not at all dangerous. However, Marilyn Church, a courtroom sketch artist present at his sanity hearing, recalled feeling very uneasy in Berkowitz's presence. He was ruled competent to stand trial and pled guilty to six murders. There was nothing untoward about his behavior until the

Most states have laws that prohibit convicted criminals from receiving financial gains related to their crimes. These laws are sometimes referred to as "Son of Sam Laws."

day of his sentencing, when Berkowitz attempted to jump out of the seventh-floor courtroom window.

Berkowitz was sentenced to six consecutive life sentences—150 years in prison. In the years since his sentencing, Berkowitz has changed his stories and apparently become religious. In 1996, Yonkers police opened an investigation into his new claims, which yielded no significant results.

Berkowitz has become eligible for parole on several occasions, but each time his plea has been rejected. Sound police work, a strong court case, and a jury's verdict saw a dangerous criminal was safely incarcerated. Mindful judicial review of his case ensures that he remains so.

The story of Son of Sam is a dramatic example of the U.S. court system at work. Not every case is as shocking as Berkowitz's was. This story does show the importance of the U.S. judicial system in keeping the citizens of America safe. But there's much more to these career choices than the inside of a courtroom. There are many opportunities for people interested contributing to the law and order of our country.

These opportunities include both positions right out there in the courtroom, on view and actively taking part in court activities, and positions that are more behind the scenes, making sure everything runs smoothly. It's important to be careful, efficient, and detail oriented. However, these jobs are key to making sure justice is served—whether that means someone goes free or someone is convicted of a crime.

These jobs include everyone from judge, prosecutor, and defense attorney to perhaps lesser-known positions such as bailiff, court clerk, court reporter, interpreter, artist, and more. If you're interested in jobs in the court system, you've come to the right place! Read on to learn more about these positions and how much education and training you need to fill them.

CHAPTER 1

THE UNITED STATES JUDICIAL SYSTEM

The U.S. Constitution defines three separate branches of government. The legislative branch proposes bills and the executive branch signs them into law. The judicial branch determines if those laws are just and constitutional, and what the appropriate sentence should be for breaking them.

At a local level, this might be a fairly simple process. If someone is accused of theft and the police have enough evidence against them, a trial will be held in a municipal courthouse. A judge or jury decides a verdict and, if guilty, hands down a suitable sentence.

Sometimes things aren't so simple. The person accused of theft will have a lawyer to represent them. Perhaps the lawyer thinks the police didn't handle the evidence for the case properly. The lawyer might decide to appeal the case—that is, to have another judge review the case and decide if the police acted correctly. The second judge might oversee several local courts. If the second judge decides that the evidence for the first case wasn't handled properly, they might overturn the first verdict.

The highest court in the United States is the Supreme Court. They don't hear the sort of cases you see on TV shows, such as *Law & Order*. Their

Courts are divided into local, state, and federal. Some questions are best decided by local authorities. Others—such as segregation and voting rights—affect all Americans.

job is to decide if laws are fair and constitutional. They don't decide if one particular person should go to jail for stealing something, but they protect everyone's rights by making sure that sentences are fair and that no one receives better treatment under the law because of their race. They make decisions that impact the laws of the entire country.

This network of courts involves judges and lawyers, but also clerks, bailiffs, translators and many other jobs. If you have an interest in serving your community and a keen mind for details, there's probably a job in the court system that's just right for you.

IS JUSTICE REALLY BLIND?

In many courtrooms and courthouses throughout America, there's a carving or image of Lady Justice. She's a tall, blindfolded woman holding a set of scales in one hand and a sword in the other. Lady Justice is a blending of several Greek goddesses that stood for justice and fairness long ago. The blindfold indicates that she's independent and impartial—she can consider both sides of an issue without bias. The scales indicate that she's weighing the evidence to see which is most truthful. And the sword shows that she has the power to enforce the law.

The figure of Lady Justice symbolizes the ideals of our society's judicial system. The system exists to set things right whenever a person has been injured, victimized, or threatened, or when one's basic civil

Laws are meant to apply equally to all citizens. No one should receive preferential treatment because of their race or financial status.

You can see bailiffs and attorneys in this picture, but it took many other people performing many different jobs to bring this case to trial.

rights have been violated. It's part of the U.S. government's great system of checks and balances. The judicial system ensures that wrong actions come with consequences. Without the justice system in place, criminals would go unpunished, victims would go unrecognized, and the concept of justice would revert to personal revenge and retaliation.

SO MANY OPTIONS

Many people are drawn to the legal system when it comes to choosing a career. A legal profession can be a noble and honorable undertaking, and being involved in the legal system is one way for people to feel as though they are making a difference in today's world. In addition, putting criminals behind bars and protecting the innocent can be exciting.

When you think of court-related jobs, you probably think of the official judge who sits up on the bench and the prosecuting and defense attorneys who battle back and forth to introduce evidence, cross-examine witnesses, or make closing arguments. However, there are far more people involved in the legal process than just a judge and two attorneys. A trial takes the coordination, skills, and hard work of a lot of people, and the jobs performed behind the scenes are some of the most important ones.

What jobs are available within the legal system other than those in the spotlight? Besides the judge, prosecuting attorney, and defense attorney, here

OTTIS TOOLE

In the American criminal justice system, a suspect is considered innocent until proven guilty. It's the responsibility of the prosecution to present a case that proves beyond a reasonable doubt that the particular suspect is guilty of the particular crime in question. In the instance of a celebrity suspect or repeat offender, jurors may be admonished to consider only the facts of the case being presented at the time.

Sometimes this process works seamlessly. The prosecution presents a compelling case with plenty of evidence that's been impeccably handled and the jury is able to reach a swift decision. In other cases, a lack of evidence or conflicting stories can prevent a case being brought to trial.

Ottis Toole (1947–1996) was a convicted serial killer considered by many law enforcement professionals to be responsible for the death of six-year-old Adam Walsh in 1981. Although the case was officially closed in 2008, Toole was never tried for the boy's death. He confessed then recanted his story multiple times, and police were unable to find Adam's body where Toole claimed it was buried. Ultimately, there wasn't enough evidence to bring a case against Toole.

As disturbing as it might be in this case, this is the way the system is supposed to work. Suspects aren't brought to trial or convicted based on their records or on stories that can't be proven with solid facts.

are some of the other important positions in the court arena:

- **Court reporter**
- **Bailiff**
- **Interpreter**
- **Courtroom sketch artist**
- **Legal secretary**
- **Law clerk**
- **Paralegal**

UNREALITY TV

Court cases have provided material for television programming since the early days of broadcasting. Generations of Americans have grown up watching crime dramas and reality courtroom shows. Many young people first develop an interest in a legal career from something they saw on TV. It's important to remember that there's a big difference between what you see on the screen and what happens every day in courthouses across the nation.

Your favorite TV dramas are fiction—made-up stories. Even ones inspired by headlines and current events alter details for dramatic effect. *Law & Order* is perhaps the most successful franchise in television history. The original program ran for 20 seasons and inspired multiple spin-off series. While perhaps more realistic than shows that came before, it's still fiction.

The *Law & Order* TV shows are considered gritty and realistic, but they show only the most dramatic moments of a case, not the tedious work performed by many people.

Real court cases, especially those that require a jury, take much longer than a single hour to resolve. Witnesses need to be interviewed. Every action taken by the police and each item of evidence must be meticulously catalogued. This sort of work can be tedious, but it's a vital part of the case.

An impartial jury must be selected. This is more difficult than it sounds. The defense attorney wants jurors who are sympathetic to their client. The district attorney wants people sympathetic to the victim. Prospective jurors might have strong opinions about the case based on what they've heard in the news . . . or they might have opinions about crime in general that could influence their judgment. An ideal jury should be a mix of ages, genders, races, and financial levels. All of these steps take more time and detail than you see in a typical television program.

Some court reality programs are closer to the actual courtroom experience. *The People's Court* and *Judge Judy* both feature actual civil cases decided by a real judge. These are real cases, but they're comparatively simple and don't require a jury. Cases are selected for the shows because they seem especially interesting or appealing to an audience. An actual day in civil court is likely to be repetitive or less entertaining.

CourtTV is a television network dedicated to coverage of high-profile criminal cases. While these are real cases, they're chosen because people have very strong feelings and opinions about them. A real-life job in the court system will always feature much

Judge Wapner (1919–2017) was a retired Los Angeles Superior Court judge who presided over real small claims court cases on *The People's Court*.

more than you see on TV. Whether you're interested in a high-profile career as a lawyer, something more active such as a bailiff, or a detailed job involving records or evidence, a career in the court system will give you the opportunity to help people and serve your community.

NOT WHAT YOU SAW ON TV

Attending a real trial is very different from watching a TV crime drama. To begin with, the process is much longer. Everything isn't wrapped up neatly in an hour. Charges need to be filed, evidence gathered, and witnesses interviewed. People and material might need to be subpoenaed—that is, ordered to appear in the court. A jury needs to be selected. There might be disagreements about the venue or courthouse where the trial will take place.

Once the trial begins, each lawyer has statements to make, evidence to present, and witnesses to call. The lawyers for both sides question each witness. Evidence will need to be explained. Once the verdict is announced, either attorney might file an appeal. If the suspect is found guilty, they will need to be sentenced. Sometimes additional civil cases follow a criminal trial. It's not uncommon for this process to take months or even years.

CHAPTER 2

THE UNSEEN HEROES OF THE COURT

Everyone has seen a courtroom on TV. There's the judge, lawyers, bailiffs, jury, and spectators. But there are many other people who do jobs necessary to a successful court case. Some might be in the courtroom—you just never really noticed them before. Others work outside the courtroom. You might never see them, but their work is equally important.

FOR THE RECORD: THE COURT REPORTER

Every official statement made in the courtroom, as well as in meetings and other legal conversations, has to be recorded. Not a single word can be missed. These records will be used as legal proof of what happened during the trial. Juries will study them. Attorneys will pore over them. These records must be completely accurate.

The person responsible for making sure every word is captured is the court reporter. The job calls for speed, accuracy, and great listening skills, as well as excellent grammar, punctuation, spelling, and a large vocabulary that includes all legal terms.

Typically, a court reporter uses a stenotype. This machine looks like an odd cross between a typewriter and a large, rather clunky adding machine. It has 22 keys on it, but unlike most keyboards, the keys are all blank. The keyboard is divided in two. The left side is called initial, and these are the keys used to record a word's first consonants. The right side is called final, and it represents the final consonants of a word. Below the two sides, in the middle, are the vowels A, O, E, and U. The keys represent sounds, and several of them are pushed at the same time to create words. Even commas and periods, along with other punctuation marks, are represented by a combination of letters.

Stenotypes used to print out paper transcripts. However, most machines now use digital memory instead. Some are connected directly to a laptop so the input is translated into text anyone can read.

In some cases, steno machines are used to do what's called real-time captioning. For this, the stenotype is directly connected to computers that translate the message so that it appears instantly

A stenotype has fewer keys than a typewriter. This is because a stenographer is recording the sounds that make up each word instead of typing each letter.

on the screen for others in the courtroom to see. (You'll read more about real-time transcriptions in chapter 5.)

Learning how to use a steno machine quickly and accurately takes time, training, and practice. It's similar to learning how to read and write a foreign language. Certified court reporters can type about 220 to 225 words per minute. (The average person speaks between 160 and 180 words a minute.)

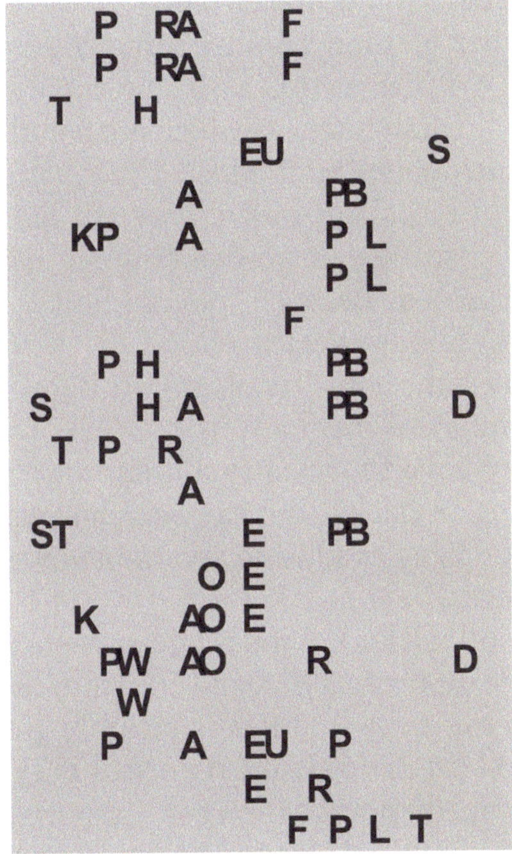

Stenotypes used to print out on paper. The transcript would then have to be translated into words that anyone can read.

Approximately 300 post-secondary vocational and technical colleges in the United States offer some kind of court reporter training. About a third of these schools are approved by the National Court Reporters Association. It takes just under three years to earn a court reporting degree. Beyond the basic training, there are additional certifications that can be earned. These include registered professional reporter, registered merit reporter, and registered diplomate reporter. Income increases as these additional certifications are earned.

Another method used by some court reporters is voice writing. In this case, the reporter speaks directly into a stenomask, which is a handheld mask with a microphone built into it. The reporter repeats every word spoken, and it is recorded. A voice silencer ensures that no one else can hear what's being repeated. Because this method is easier, it takes only about a year to learn.

While some court reporters work for law firms, a great many of them are freelancers. This means they may have to travel to a different place every day. Being on call like this can be a challenge, but for some who like flexible and spontaneous schedules, it's perfect.

The outlook for this job is fantastic—skilled court reporters are in great demand. The number of court cases in the United States is steadily growing, so the need for reliable court reporters is expected to rise. The median wage for a court reporter is about $60,000 per year. If a person likes to type, can pay

A stenomask is connected directly to a voice writing computer program. It's faster and easier to learn than a stenotype. However, a court reporter is supposed to be unobtrusive, and a stenomask is very noticeable.

a great deal of attention to detail, and has sharp listening skills, then a court reporter job may be ideal. Reporters are paid for the hours they spend at the steno machine in the courtroom, and they're also paid for each page they translate into text. (A typical six-hour steno session results in about 250 pages of text.) The job isn't a difficult one physically, with the only possible problems being fatigue from sitting in the same position for hours and carpal tunnel syndrome from repetitive movements.

THE EVOLUTION OF THE STENOTYPE MACHINE

The very first stenotype machine was patented in 1879 by Miles Bartholomew. The machine printed out shorthand onto a strip of paper. Only someone trained in stenography or shorthand could understand what it said. The shorthand printout would then be transcribed into full words and punctuation that anyone could read. This would become part of the records of the court case.

Over time, the machines were redesigned. They became more sophisticated and easier to use. In 1963, the first model of stenotype machine that could be connected to a computer with a cable was introduced. In 1987 a new model encoded directly onto a floppy disc and in 1992 the first stenotype capable of instantaneous translation of text became available.

KEEPING THINGS SAFE: THE BAILIFF

In America, the job of protecting the people in the courtroom belongs to the bailiff. The bailiff's job begins before anyone even enters the room. They look through the courtroom, checking to make sure it's clear of any weapons or bombs. They also check to see if the room is clean and ready for use.

Bailiffs perform a variety of tasks that keep the courtroom running smoothly. Today this often includes telling people to turn off and put away their cell phones.

Once the court session begins, the bailiff really goes to work. They maintain order in the courtroom, informing everyone present of the courtroom rules and making sure all the rules are enforced. The bailiff announces the arrival of the judge, calls witnesses to the stand, and often swears them in. They handle evidence and escort the defendant to and from the courtroom. The bailiff is responsible for checking everyone who walks into the courtroom for a weapon and restraining anyone who's uncooperative or hostile. They then have the right to remove or even arrest the person. It's their job to contact medical help if necessary, or call for additional security.

For some trials, the juries must be quarantined, or sequestered, meaning the members can't go back home at the end of the day. Instead, they're required to stay in a court-appointed hotel. They even have to eat at restaurants chosen by the court. When this happens, the bailiff escorts the jury members from one place to the next, and protects them while they're sequestered. If the media or any other unauthorized people attempt to speak to jurors, the bailiff intervenes.

Bailiffs are required to carry a gun. They have to be physically fit so they can chase someone or wrestle someone out of the room. Technically, a person is qualified for the job of bailiff if they have a high school diploma or General Educational Development (GED) credential. However, the chances of getting a job are much better for those with a degree in law enforcement or criminal justice. Some bailiffs start off as sheriffs' deputies or police officers. Certain states require applicants to take the state's Peace Officers Standards and Training (POST) course, which sets selection and training standards for law enforcement officials. First-aid and self-defense skills are necessary for this job, as well as knowledge of gun safety. The median pay for a bailiff is about $48,000 per year.

WHAT DID THEY SAY? THE INTERPRETER

Imagine how frightening and confusing it would be to be called to the witness stand to swear to "tell the truth, the whole truth, and nothing but the truth" in a language that wasn't familiar. For witnesses who don't speak English or who are hearing impaired, this is exactly what happens. Language difficulties can certainly create problems in trials, meetings, depositions, interviews, and witness preparation. This is where the court interpreter comes into the picture.

The job of the court interpreter is to relay messages to a person in a language the person can understand. In addition to translating the literal meaning of the words, the interpreter must be able to impart the message without any additions, omissions, or alterations to the meaning. For some, this means translating English into another language; for others, it means translating spoken language into sign language.

Naturally, a court interpreter must know at least two languages at a native or mastery level. The primary language needed for interpretation in today's courts is Spanish, followed by Chinese, Portuguese, Vietnamese, Korean, Russian, and Arabic. Sign language interpreters are in high demand as well. They must be experts in American Sign Language (ASL), knowing the grammar rules, sentence structures, and idioms the language uses. Interpreters who also know tactile signing—used for someone who's both deaf and blind—are in even greater demand.

Translators ensure that anyone involved in a case can understand what's being said. They also make it possible for witnesses to communicate their testimony, regardless of what language they speak.

Some court interpreters work in teams of two. This way, if the proceedings go on for a long time, one person can relieve the other. One also serves as backup for the other in case a term is misunderstood or needs clarification.

To prove a person is qualified as a court interpreter, he or she is usually required to take a written examination that tests proficiency in both languages. Often, this is combined with a practical or oral exam. Currently, federal court certification for interpreters is available in Spanish.

Because interpreters are hard to find, they're in great demand. Those who are certified make substantially more income than those who aren't. In fact, a certified interpreter will earn almost double what an uncertified interpreter makes for the same type of work. The work environment can be demanding and stressful, but since many interpreters work freelance, they may also enjoy a great deal of variety in their work. The median income for an interpreter is about $52,000 per year.

WHAT'S HAPPENING IN THERE? THE SKETCH ARTIST

The topic of media presence in courtrooms has long been a subject of debate in the United States. Some people feel it falls under the First Amendment protections for a free press. They believe the public has a right to see the judicial system in operation.

One of the arguments against cameras in the courtroom is that they can distract or even cause distress to witnesses giving testimony. A single sketch artist is much more discreet.

Others argue that the people involved in the trial are entitled to a fair trial and a measure of privacy—after all, they're innocent until proven guilty. Court officers have found photographers to be a distraction in the courtroom.

The media circus surrounding the 1935 trial of Bruno Hauptmann, who eventually was convicted and executed for the kidnapping and murder of Charles Lindbergh's baby son, resulted in the prohibition of cameras from American courtrooms. Since then, there have been small pilot programs in different states to see how cameras might be reintroduced to the courtroom. Through all of this, the major source of trial images has been the courtroom sketch artist.

This can be an intriguing career option for someone with artistic talent and an interest in the judicial system. A courtroom sketch artist must be able to work unobtrusively from their assigned seat in the courtroom with a small assortment of tools. This might include binoculars if their seat is far from the main participants of the trial!

Artists also must follow any directions given by the judge or bailiffs. This can include being asked to remove images of the jury from their sketches, having their sketches confiscated, or even being escorted out of the courtroom.

Courtroom sketch artists must have a keen eye for capturing the emotional impact of pivotal moments in a trial. They must be able to work quickly and the subjects of their sketches must be instantly recognizable. Unlike other types of commissions, which an artist can take time to complete in a studio, courtroom sketch artists work under tight deadlines. Their sketches are often turned in during breaks in the trial for broadcast on that evening's news.

Courtroom sketch artists often work freelance and they're often hired by the press. This means they're able to do other kinds of work. This can be helpful for them, as working every day in the high security atmosphere of a courthouse can be stress-

After being printed or broadcast on the news media, original courtroom sketches might be exhibited as part of a museum collection.

ful. Covering a trial can expose them to upsetting testimony and evidence.

Working as a court sketch artist is a unique opportunity to share the way our judicial system works with people outside the courtroom. According to the Bureau of Labor Statistics, the median pay for craft and fine artists was $48,760 per year in 2019. However, freelancers might make less.

MARILYN CHURCH

Marilyn Church has captured some of the most famous court cases of the 20th century with her sketches. From being unnervingly close to David Berkowitz to the graphic evidence of the Central Park Jogger case to Marla Maples's shoes, she's seen it all—and sketched it for the press and for posterity.

More than 4,500 of her sketches are in the collection of the Library of Congress. Others are held by the Smithsonian. Her sketches have appeared in *The New York Times* and many major television networks. Some are published in a book entitled *The Art of Justice*. Many of her drawings are instantly recognizable images of celebrities during their moments in court. Others capture intense moments of raw emotion.

CHAPTER 3

EVERYONE KNOWS WHO THAT IS

Anyone who's seen a legal or crime drama on television can recognize the main people in a courtroom. The judge with their robe and gavel oversees the room from their elevated bench. The two groups of attorneys—prosecution and defense—don't wear special clothing, like the judge, but they're easily recognizable from their places at the two tables in front of the bench.

These three are the key players in our judicial system. Anyone accused of a crime is entitled to competent legal counsel, even if they can't afford it. The victim of a crime is usually represented by the state, in the form of a district attorney. The judge presides over their activity in the court-

Judge Mary Bartelme of Illinois was the first female judge in the United States. She presided over Children's Night Court. Today, there are women judges in all American courts, including the U.S. Supreme Court.

room. They ensure that information is presented fairly so the jury can make a good decision.

SITTING IN JUDGMENT

The judge in a courtroom is in a position of power, control, and immense importance. As a popular superhero once stated, "With great power comes great responsibility." This is certainly true for all the nation's judges, at both the federal and state levels. Being a respected and trustworthy judge takes a combination of skills. You need compassion and

THE GREAT DISSENTER

Oliver Wendell Holmes Jr. (1841–1935) is perhaps the most famous name in American judicial history. He served as a captain in the Union Army during the Civil War. He graduated from Harvard Law School in 1866 and later taught law there.

In 1902, President Theodore Roosevelt nominated Holmes to the U.S. Supreme Court. He would serve as an associate justice for nearly 30 years. Holmes was known as the Great Dissenter for his carefully reasoned minority opinions.

He's probably best known for his opinions on the First Amendment. He established the standard of "clear and present" danger being the only legitimate reason to curtail a person's freedom of speech. His often-quoted example is: "The most stringent protection of free speech would not protect a man in falsely shouting fire in a theater and causing a panic."

Harvard Law School celebrated its bicentennial in 2018. It's produced more Supreme Court Justices than any other law school, including Oliver Wendell Holmes.

objectivity but also the ability to listen carefully and ponder decisions slowly. Above all, you need the inner conviction that any person is innocent until proven guilty and that everyone, regardless of the crime, deserves a fair trial. This isn't a job for the type of person who always has to be up and running around. It's for the person who can sit, listen, analyze, and, of course, judge.

Judges have been trained for years to preside over trials and hearings and to make sure every trial is fair. They know how laws can and can't be applied, and they oversee the legal process as a whole. A judge rules on the admissibility of evidence. Will it or will it not be allowed during testimony? Will it be shown to the jury? It's up to the judge to decide.

If attorneys go too far in their examinations or push the boundaries of the law, the judge interrupts the proceedings to restore order. If the attorneys start arguing over a point, the judge steps in and reminds them how to behave in a court of law—and punishes them if they don't cooperate. A judge is like a teacher in a large classroom, making sure all rules are followed, all procedures are properly performed, and all parties are doing their jobs correctly.

Other job duties include instructing the jury on how to reach a verdict and listening to allegations and charges at pretrial hearings to decide if there's enough evidence to merit an actual trial. If there is, the judge also determines if the person can be released on bail (and the amount) or if he or she should be kept in prison until the trial officially

Not every trial is for a famous crime. TV shows such as *Judge Judy* and *The People's Court* show the types of cases judges preside over every day in courtrooms across the country.

begins. For a bench trial, or a trial for which there is no jury, the judge alone determines the verdict of guilty or not guilty.

Of course, judges perform work outside the courtroom too. In their offices and in law libraries, they read documents, research judicial issues, and write opinions. They may work 50 or more hours a week.

Judges in federal courts are appointed by the president of the United States and are confirmed by a Senate vote. For the past few decades, all of the jus-

RBG

Ruth Bader Ginsburg (1933–2020) was an associate justice of the U.S. Supreme Court. She's remembered for her work to overcome gender discrimination. She didn't just argue for women's rights, but also men's rights in cases where men had been discriminated against for taking on roles that society traditionally assigned to women.

As a student at Harvard, she was one of nine female students in a class of 500. She was famously accused of taking a spot at Harvard Law School that might have gone to a male student. When her husband accepted a job at a New York City law firm, she transferred to Columbia Law School. She graduated at the top of her class in 1959 and later returned to Columbia to teach, becoming the first female professor to earn tenure.

Judge Ginsburg headed the American Civil Liberties Union's (ACLU) Women's Rights Project in the 1970s. In 1980, President Jimmy Carter appointed her to the U.S. Court of Appeals for the District of Columbia and in 1993, President Bill Clinton nominated her to the U.S. Supreme Court, where she served until her death.

Ruth Bader Ginsburg was a hero and role model for a lot of people. Many people mourned her when she died in 2020.

tices appointed to serve on the U.S. Supreme Court were previously federal court judges. On the state level, about half the judges are appointed, while the other half are voted in through statewide elections.

It takes a great deal of experience to become a judge. State and federal judges typically spend years as lawyers first. The job of judge requires a person who can maintain a constant level of impartiality, has an in-depth understanding of laws, has the ability to sit patiently and listen carefully for many hours at a time, and is able to make final, serious decisions based on hard evidence—decisions that have the potential to change, or even end, a person's life.

ARGUING FOR A LIVING

With so many lawyers in movies, on television, and in books, it seems like most people would know what it takes to become an attorney. The job is often glamorized, however, and what's seen on television is rarely an accurate representation of what the job involves. If you love to argue or debate, then becoming a lawyer may be a great career choice. Lawyers are certainly the ones in the spotlight during a trial, so someone who doesn't feel comfortable in that position, who is shy or self-conscious, or who's simply not at his or her best in front of a crowd would be better off pursuing a different legal job.

The first step in becoming an attorney is getting a four-year college degree. While there's no official pre-law curriculum a student must take as an undergraduate, experts do recommend that prospective lawyers become proficient in certain areas. These include writing, public speaking, reading, and logical analysis. It's also a good idea to take classes in foreign languages, government, history, philosophy, political science, and computer science.

Becoming a lawyer requires two college degrees. This is a very serious commitment of time, effort, and money.

Judicial Firsts

- James McDonald, first Native American professionally trained as a lawyer, circa 1820s
- Macon Bolling Allen, first African American lawyer and judge, admitted to the Massachusetts Bar 1844, Massachusetts Justice of the Peace 1848, elected South Carolina Probate Court Judge 1874
- Arabella A. Mansfield, first female lawyer in America 1869
- Charlotte E. Ray, first female African American lawyer 1872
- Jane Bolin, first African American woman to graduate from Yale Law School 1931, sworn to the New York City Bench 1939
- Thurgood Marshall, first African American Supreme Court Justice 1967
- Ruth Bader Ginsburg, first female tenured law professor, Columbia University 1972
- Marilyn Church, female courtroom sketch artist, late 20th century
- Sandra Day O'Connor, first female Supreme Court Justice 1981
- Sonia Sotomayor, first Hispanic Federal Judge in New York 1992, nominated to the Supreme Court 2009
- Diane Humetewa, first female Native American Federal Judge 2014

After graduation from college, students apply to law schools. Whether or not they're accepted depends on a combination of factors, including grade average, prior work experience, and their performance on the LSAT, or Law School Admissions Test. Some schools also require a personal interview with the applicant. Competition is intense, especially for the top schools, and there are always more applicants than there are openings.

If a student is accepted, then it's time for three years of law school. The better law schools are accredited by the American Bar Association (ABA), meaning the school's faculty, library, and classes meet set standards. In 2020, there were 203 ABA approved law schools throughout the United States.

The first half of law school is spent taking core courses such as constitutional law, contracts and torts, and research and legal documents. Over the second half of law school, students decide which kind of law they want to specialize in. They also spend this time getting practical experience in legal clinics and taking part in mock scenarios and trials, along with researching and writing for the school's law journal.

There are several different types of lawyers. Law students may choose to go into criminal or civil law, and they may decide to be a defense attorney or a prosecutor. In addition, they may work through a law firm or in a private practice.

INNOCENT UNTIL PROVEN GUILTY

A defense attorney advocates for the accused, working on the important legal principle that the accused is innocent until proven guilty. The defense attorney reviews the case and seeks evidence and witnesses to corroborate the defendant's story.

Some defense attorneys can be pro bono lawyers or public defenders. Both types of lawyers provide free legal help for clients who are unable to pay for their services.

The state pays the salary of a public defender, which is appointed by the court for defendants who can't afford to pay for private counsel. It's a very demanding job, with these lawyers commonly handling 30 to 40 cases at a time.

Some private legal offices also perform pro bono work, with lawyers volunteering their time and efforts. Pro bono coordinators or managers communicate with courts and public interest organizations to help provide qualified legal services for deserving individuals or organizations. In addition, experienced coordinators often provide support and training for lawyers handling individual pro bono legal cases. The Association of Pro Bono Counsel is an organization that supports pro bono legal services.

One of the foundations of our legal system is the idea that anyone accused of a crime is entitled to qualified legal counsel, regardless of their financial circumstances.

BUILDING A SOLID CASE

A prosecuting attorney is responsible for presenting the case in a criminal trial against an individual suspected of breaking the law. The prosecutor is the legal representative of the jurisdiction (state, county, or district, for example) in which the alleged crime took place.

The prosecutor often visits the crime scene, reviews evidence, interviews witnesses, requests additional tests from forensics, and prepares for trial. Viktor Theiss, a prosecuting attorney in Massachusetts, described his job on Frontline: "It's the best job I've ever had. I love being a DA [district attorney]. At the end of the day, I get to go home and know that I accomplished something and that there are so many times during the day when I'm making these massive decisions about whether we should prosecute, if we do prosecute, what should the sentence be, and I'm working with people that, but for my efforts, would have no voice—victims of domestic violence, child victims, some of the elderly, just people in the community. It's a great mission to know that when you go to work, you're not just working for some kind of corporate entity, one individual's wishes—but that you have this higher principle that you act according to."

Theiss went on to impart some advice to those students considering a career as a prosecuting attorney: "If you really want to be a good DA, I think you have to really begin focusing on developing

An attorney of any sort has to be good with attention to detail. Courtroom attorneys must be good at working with people too. They have a very important job.

interpersonal skills, learning how to interact with a wide variety of people. You want to really study in law school some of the underlying procedures and the law that governs them." He added, "While you're an undergrad, taking some courses on the criminal justice system will give you a huge leg up. Understanding some of the societal factors that are involved in crime is huge ... in general, having life experiences that take you outside what your normal role may be."

THE MOST FAMILIAR TYPE OF LAWYER

When most people hear the word "lawyer," the first thing they picture is the criminal lawyer. Whether on the prosecuting or defense side, being a criminal lawyer takes a combination of determination, commitment, knowledge, patience, and an ability to work well with a lot of people. Typically, these lawyers handle such crimes as:

- Traffic violations
- Petty theft
- Possession of drugs
- Rape
- Grand theft
- Assault and battery
- Assault with a deadly weapon
- Homicide/murder

The trials for these crimes involve many people, so a criminal lawyer needs to be a real team player.

DIFFERENT TYPES OF LAW DEGREES

The law schools accredited by the American Bar Association award the juris doctorate (JD) degree. This is a post-graduate professional degree that prepares students to take their state's bar exam. This degree sometimes is called the first degree, as it is required to practice law.

The other law degree available is the master of laws (LLM). This is a secondary degree that a lawyer might choose to pursue after achieving their JD and passing the bar. An LLM signifies that a lawyer has made extensive study of a particular legal specialty.

The United States Army Judge Advocate General's School is accredited by the ABA, despite offering only the LLM and not the JD degree. This is due to the specialized nature of the school.

SO MUCH MORE

Although the criminal lawyer is the one most familiar from TV and novels, there are many other ways to practice law. Unlike a criminal lawyer, a civil lawyer focuses on such legal documents as wills, trusts, contracts, titles, and leases. Civil law, as opposed to criminal law, settles disputes in which money (compensation) may be awarded to the victim(s). A number of specialties are available for civil lawyers, depending on their passions and interests. These specialties include:

- Bankruptcy law
- Environmental law
- Family law
- Intellectual property law
- Probate law
- Real estate law
- Insurance law
- International law
- Elder law

Regardless of which type of legal practice interests you, one trait necessary to being a lawyer is a love of learning. In addition to a four-year college degree and three years of law school to achieve a JD, there's still more to learn.

In order to be a practicing attorney, it's necessary for a prospective lawyer to pass the bar exam for the jurisdiction where they wish to practice. This is a two-day exam composed of separate tests in varying formats, including multiple choice and essay. The bar exam tests an applicant's knowledge of many facets of law that were covered in school.

In addition, most states require prospective lawyers to pass the Multistate Professional Responsibility Examination (MPRE). This exam tests the applicant's understanding of the standards of professional conduct expected of practicing attorneys. Admission to the bar might also require passing an ethics tests or interview, a thorough background check, and fingerprinting.

Even after being admitted to the bar, there's still more to learn. A lawyer might choose to become more specialized and pursue their LLM degree. Most states require lawyers to complete a certain amount of continuing education each year. New laws are constantly being written and old ones struck down or reinterpreted.

CHAPTER 4

THE LEGAL WORK BEHIND THE SCENES

When you walk into a courtroom, you see lawyers who have come prepared to present their case. They have their evidence and notes organized and they've practiced their arguments. They will each present their case and the judge will make a decision.

What you don't see are all the people who helped the lawyers and judge prepare for their courtroom appearance. Documents have to be typed to specific formats. Some might need to be notarized. Many things will need to be copied and filed. Evidence might need to be formatted for presentation. Research needs to be done on the specific laws involved in the case and what decisions were made in similar cases.

Former U.S. Attorney Preet Bharara is presenting information during a press conference. Someone in his office organized the information, formatted this chart, and arranged to have it printed.

LEGAL SECRETARY

One of the most influential positions in the entire legal system is that of legal secretary. This person often is the first one you meet when dealing with a legal firm or attorney's office. The secretary is the one who relays phone calls, delivers messages, schedules appointments, and generally makes sure that the boss is in the right place at the right time. It's no surprise that some legal secretaries are better known as information managers.

A legal secretary's job often encompasses the basic clerical duties of most office secretaries, but it's also often much more specialized. The legal secretary must conduct some legal research, create spreadsheets and multimedia presentations, and provide materials requested by the attorney, paralegal, or legal assistant. A great amount of office time is spent preparing and proofreading various legal documents, such as legal invoices, deposition notices, pleadings, briefs, and subpoenas. Another big responsibility is keeping a legal or trial calendar, complete with legal filing deadlines, hearings, meetings, and closings. Deadlines in the legal system are extremely important, as filing a form one day late or forgetting to respond to one can jeopardize an entire case.

Anyone interested in the job of legal secretary should be extremely organized and know how to pay attention to detail in the midst of chaos. Fast and up-to-date computer skills are essential, as is

A legal secretary is trained to do the same sort of tasks as any other office professional, but with extra training for working in a legal environment.

knowing how to meet the multiple daily needs of clients and employers. Excellent spelling, grammar, and punctuation skills are vital.

The National Association for Legal Professionals offers certificates to those who pass special exams. There are two certifications: Accredited Legal Professional and Certified Legal Professional. The job outlook for this position is good and is expected to remain so in the foreseeable future.

KEEPING THE COURTROOM ORDERLY

Another clerical job that's necessary to the system is the court clerk. Court clerks have been described as the oil that keeps the court's engine running smoothly. A good court clerk is a person who can multitask, jumping from one duty to another seamlessly. Being able to process paperwork efficiently is helpful; being able to follow up on missing paperwork and other obstacles is mandatory. Clerks keep quite busy with a long list of duties. Once a case has been scheduled on the calendar, the court clerk sends a letter to those participating in the process, announcing when and where the trial will be held. Next, the clerk prepares a folder for the case and then, over time, adds relevant documents to it.

After a legal document is submitted to the court, the clerk is responsible for checking it for accuracy. If there's a mistake, the clerk goes back to the person who completed the form and explains the problem. Just before a case begins, the clerk checks the case

Court clerks must be knowledgeable about the types of documents required for a court case. It's their job to ensure all the paperwork is present and correct before a hearing.

folder to make sure all of the pertinent paperwork is enclosed. If something is missing, the clerk has to track it down.

In addition to helping lawyers, court clerks assist judges by contacting witnesses and preparing any forms the judge might need during a hearing or trial. When a case is under way in the courtroom, it's often the court clerk who swears in the jurors and witnesses. Court clerks also keep track of case results, court orders, and unpaid fees. They collect court fees or fines, as well as bail payments, and make sure the amount is recorded properly. Typically, clerks also are responsible for filing public records, such as mortgages, deeds, and marriage licenses. A court clerk often is given the responsibility of maintaining custody of trial evidence and numbering and labeling it for identification.

You can become a court clerk with a high school diploma or certificate of General Educational Development (GED). However, your chances of landing a job are better if you also have at least two years of college or business school. A bachelor's degree is helpful. To be a federal court clerk, you're expected to have a master's degree or law degree. Clearly, all English language skills must be excellent, as well as familiarity with word processing, bookkeeping, accounting, and business management. A court clerk might expect to earn about $40,000 per year.

ASSISTING THE JUDGE

Law clerks, who are usually attorneys, work closely with a judge to help him or her make informed legal decisions. They help in courtroom proceedings through their various interactions with the court's staff, the litigants, and the general public. The law clerk helps the judge review briefs, verify legal authority, perform legal research, and write various legal documents. Law clerks in appellate courts focus on research and the legal issues involved in appeals. In addition, before the proceedings begin, law clerks inform the judge and the judge's staff about the highlights of a case. This position is an influential one because a judge's decision may be guided by a clerk's recommendations.

Most law clerks are recent law school graduates who take a one- or two-year clerkship with a judge. Usually, only the students with the highest grades are chosen for clerkships because there are only a few select openings. Anyone pursuing this position should have excellent communication skills, strong research skills, and a very thorough understanding of all aspects of court procedures, legal rules, and the court system. Unlike trial attorneys, law clerks don't have to stand up in court, although they still do research, make decisions, and are completely involved in the judicial process. Federal law clerks make a higher annual salary than state law clerks.

BLAZING A TRAIL

For nearly a century after the founding of the United States, the law was considered a man's profession. This changed in 1869 when Arabella Mansfield was admitted to the Iowa bar, becoming the first female lawyer in the United States. That same year, Myra Bradwell passed the bar exam, but the state of Illinois refused to admit her to the bar on the basis of her gender. The Illinois Supreme Court reversed that decision in 1890.

These women helped pave the way for Charlotte E. Ray and Jane Bolin, the first African American women to become a lawyer and a judge, respectively. They were followed by the appointments of Sandra Day O'Connor and Ruth Bader Ginsburg as associate justices of the U.S. Supreme Court in the late 20th century. In 2009, Sonia Sotomayor became the first Hispanic judge appointed to the U.S. Supreme Court.

Myra Bradwell was admitted to the bar in the state of Illinois, decades before women were allowed to vote.

ASSISTING ATTORNEYS

Perhaps you're fascinated by the law and the intricacy of legal procedures, but don't like public speaking or being the center of attention. Maybe you're a person who's more skilled at preparation than presentation. A career as a paralegal might be a good choice for you. Paralegals can do most of the things lawyers do except for setting fees, presenting a case in court, or giving legal advice.

Paralegals assist attorneys in many ways. They conduct research necessary for a case and organize it for the lawyer to study. They interview clients and witnesses. They draft arguments for lawyers and prepare legal documents such as wills.

Most paralegals work in law firms, in corporate legal departments, or for government offices. They often specialize in a specific area, such as:

- Litigation
- Personal injury
- Corporate law
- Criminal law
- Employee benefits
- Intellectual property
- Labor law
- Bankruptcy
- Immigration
- Real estate
- Family law

A paralegal tends to do their work in an office or library setting, rather than a courtroom. Their work is still invaluable to the process of criminal justice.

Some paralegals also work for nonprofit or civil rights organizations such as the American Civil Liberties Union (ACLU) or the National Association for the Advancement of Colored People (NAACP). This type of work can be deeply satisfying on a personal level.

There's currently no national standard of education or certification required for employment as a paralegal. Requirements vary by state. Generally, at least a two-year college degree is necessary, with a four-year degree being preferred. Currently, the American Bar Association (ABA) approves 260 programs. Various professional organizations offer certificate programs for paralegals, in addition to the required college degree. A paralegal might expect to earn about $52,000 per year. This is a rapidly expanding career field.

STEPPING STONE

Sometimes, people become paralegals with an eye toward using the job as a stepping stone toward becoming an attorney. After all, after a few years working as a paralegal, you'll have a lot of experience that other law school students don't have! This might (or might not) be a good path for you. While a background as a paralegal won't necessarily make your law school application more likely to get you in, your experience in the field could very well help you do great once you're in law school.

There are a number of things to consider first, however. While attorneys make more money than paralegals, law school is also much more expensive. And while a paralegal may be able to have a two-year degree in some states, you will still need a bachelor's degree to apply to law school. Also, paralegals often get paid for overtime (attorneys don't) and tend to have a better work-life balance.

Of course, time as a paralegal before moving on to law school can also help you decide if you even want to go on to become an attorney. It could be a good way to find out if you like the field enough before you spend a significant amount of money on a law degree.

Becominng a paralegal is hard work, but it can be the perfect starting point when pursuing a career in law.

10 GREAT QUESTIONS TO ASK A PARALEGAL

1. What kind of schooling did you need for this job?
2. How much did that schooling cost?
3. Could this job be a step toward a different legal career?
4. What's a typical day in your job look like?
5. Do you have to be in the courtroom at all?
6. What do you specialize in?
7. What's your favorite part of your job?
8. What's your least favorite part of your job?
9. What kind of research do you do?
10. Do you feel like your job helps people?

CHAPTER 5

TECHNOLOGY IN THE COURTROOM

Even prior to the global pandemic of 2020, courtrooms were becoming more technologically advanced. A PowerPoint slideshow is more visible and more clearly understood than photocopies or diagrams drawn on a whiteboard. Having an expert witness testify via video call is much easier and less expensive than having them travel from a remote location.

In 2020, the legal field, like so many other industries, was suddenly forced to rely even more heavily on computer and internet technology to conduct business safely. Faced with a situation in which it was unsafe to physically gather large groups of people together, but bound by the Sixth Amendment guarantee of a speedy trial by jury,

Video screens in the jury box ensure that all jurors have a clear view of evidence being presented.

the courts turned to technology to conduct business remotely. More paperwork was filed via email and teleconferences or video conferencing programs such as Skype were used for virtual court appearances.

THE LATEST IN EVIDENCE PRESENTATION

Installing a digital evidence presentation system (DEPS) in a courtroom helps speed up procedures and cut down on paperwork and waste. This system allows judges and lawyers to show evidence and other case documents to jurors on a set of large flat-screen monitors mounted throughout the courtroom, including in the jury box, witness box, judge's bench, courtroom reporter station, courtroom deputy station, and at counsel tables. When the evidence or document is displayed on the screens, an attorney or a witness can use an illustrator or annotation pen to highlight a small detail or unusual marking.

The DEPS is designed so that all exhibits are easy to see. It can display almost any type of courtroom evidence, including documents, three-dimensional objects, photographs, X-rays, negatives, slideshow and PowerPoint presentations, charts and graphs, and transparencies. While most of these images can be seen by the courtroom audience as well, the judge has a "kill switch" at the bench to immediately blank out certain screens if necessary. Judge Catherine Perry of Missouri explains, "The judge is always in control of the trial just like before. I realized all I needed was that one switch that turns off the jury

Technology like this helps everyone in a courtroom see the evidence they need to see. It can help keep things running smoothly.

monitors. I can still decide whether evidence is more prejudicial than probative. And I can control how many photographs get shown if we have an accident scene or injury site. My job as a judge has not changed. I still control what the jury sees and how much they see of it."

The DEPS is considered the control center. It's typically built inside a console known as a media cart. The DEPS usually includes a document camera and a touchscreen monitor so lawyers can easily incorporate changing screens into their speeches or examination questions. The system is also designed so laptops can be plugged into it. Chief Judge Rodney Webb of North Dakota says this new technology is really helping the court save time. "In the past, in trials with a lot of papers or trials that had a lot of pictures," he says, "you had to publish these things and distribute them to the jury. Now, we publish all pictures and written documents received in evidence through the monitors, and it saves enormous amounts of time." Judge James Gwin from Ohio also appreciates the amount of time saved using the DEPS. "In most cases, I estimate that it moves things along 30 percent faster," he states. "In a traditional trial, there is so much dead time with lawyers shuffling papers for witnesses' examination. Even when exhibit books are used, there's time taken to get the witness to the right pages, the right paragraph." The DEPS also includes a high-quality DVD player with freeze-frame capability so the court can see recordings frame by frame.

WEBCAMS IN THE COURTROOM

One key technological change that's taken place relatively recently is the ability to conduct video conferences in the courtroom. This technology uses video to allow witnesses who are off-site to give "live" testimony during a trial. Video conferencing saves time and money because witnesses don't have to travel from faraway locations to testify in a courtroom.

Chief bankruptcy Judge Lee Jackwig from Iowa finds video conferencing quite helpful. She describes

During the 2020 pandemic, it wasn't safe for people to gather. Much of the business of the courts was conducted via video conferencing platforms such as Skype or Zoom.

how when she's listening to testimony from the witness stand, she typically can see only the back of the speaker's head or a profile. "But a witness testifying [by video conference] is pretty much facing me on the screen," she explains. "I have a very good view of that individual and can watch the facial expression, mannerism, etc., that go into judging credibility."

Legal scholar and U.S. Court of Appeals Judge Guido Calabresi was very reluctant to use this new technology. "I am one of those antediluvian people who still do everything in old-fashioned ways," he admits. "I don't use a computer . . . so when I heard about that video conferencing, I wouldn't say I was sure it wouldn't work, but I was very skeptical." However, after using it a short time, Judge Calabresi changed his mind. "It worked out very well. I've had no problems with it at all," he says. "And more than that, I had a sense that people have been able to make their arguments in a way that is more relaxed than if they had to come rushing down from a long distance."

In addition, advanced audio equipment, such as audio enhancement and infrared headphones, has been added to the courtroom to help those who are hearing impaired. Such technology also makes it easier for everyone in the courtroom to hear hard-to-understand audio evidence, such as undercover tapes.

CLOSED CAPTIONING IN THE COURTROOM

One of the biggest recent advances in courtroom procedure is the development of real-time transcriptions. For these, the court reporter uses the stenographer machine as usual to record everything that's said. But, instead of the transcript being translated later, the information is immediately converted to text that can be seen on computer monitors, or television or projection screens. Court reporter Ed Hawkins from Washington, D.C., says, "Real-time combines writing, translating, and editing into a single function."

THE MOST ADVANCED COURTROOM IN THE WORLD

William and Mary Law School in Williamsburg, Virginia, is home to the Center for Legal and Court Technology (CLCT). A major goal of the project is to test the latest commercially available technology in a real courtroom. The McGlothlin Courtroom is equipped with the latest computer and video technology. The center provides support to court systems around the country that seek to upgrade their judicial facilities.

In addition to the practical use of technology in the courtroom, the center researches cybercrimes and the ethical use of technology by the justice system. They host conferences on many topics related to the use of technology in the court system.

Technology is a big part of courtrooms these days, and it can make things much easier, but some things remain the same.

Computer-assisted real-time transcription, or CART, was originally designed to help those with hearing impairments. It has since expanded. Now, it's used with jurors, plaintiffs, defendants, and attorneys in conferences, meetings, and trials. By seeing what was said only seconds after it was said, attorneys can mark the places they might want to return to during later questioning or closing procedures. All they have to do is press the space bar on their laptops, and the system inserts a reference mark. At the end of the day, attorneys can also go home with a rough draft of everything that was said, rather than waiting a few hours or a day. This helps them prepare for the next day's court session, thus improving efficiency.

Since real-time transcriptions can be safely sent across the Internet, experts can monitor testimony as it's being given, no matter their location. This way, they can write down questions or responses for later discussion. Judges also find advantages to real-time transcriptions. They have an instant copy to help them deal with difficult motions and rulings, they can better understand witnesses who might have a speech impediment or strong accent, and they can better review a question to a witness and then rule on a lawyer's objection to it. Judge James Robertson from the U.S. District Court for the District of Columbia says CART helps him focus more on the trial. "The need to take notes is not as important," he points out.

Another reason the electronic courtroom is growing in popularity is simple: With today's juries, the electronic medium is often the best way to communicate. For example, many young jury members are used to getting the majority of their news, information, and entertainment via the internet. Those accustomed to the net's colorful graphics, bulleted lists, and brief sound bites may actually struggle to remain focused when faced with nothing but two attorneys and their note cards. Such jury members may find themselves daydreaming instead of concentrating—something that could certainly turn the course of a trial when it comes to reaching a verdict. As Judge Ben Tennille from the North Carolina Business Court puts it, "We get most of our information off of a screen these days, whether it's a computer screen, a television screen, or an iPhone screen. That's the way jurors want their information."

Although CART is helpful, not all court reporters know how to use it and not all judges will allow it in their courtrooms. Daryl Teshima, an attorney, writes, "Real-time requires a court reporter that can instantly turn a cacophony of voices into coherent, mistake-free text. There is no opportunity for the reporter to review a tape of the proceedings or clean up the rough transcript. If the court reporter is not up to speed, the ensuing transcript will probably be useless." While CART is not necessarily for everyone, for others, it's ideal. "Real-time reporting works because it represents the best of two worlds: the skill

Courthouses need qualified IT professionals to ensure that equipment is properly installed and legal professionals know how to use it.

IN THE TIME OF COVID-19

On May 4, 2020, the U.S. Supreme Court broadcast oral arguments live for the first time in its history. This took place because of the COVID-19 pandemic, but the change had other implications as well. Only a very limited number of seats are usually available to watch the court live, but this opened up the proceedings to everyone with technological access.Advocates for great court transparency hailed the change as a positive move.

Not all the courtroom changes due to COVID were without their issues, however. That same month, Texas held its first jury trial via Zoom, a video-conferencing system many people relied on during the pandemic. However, one juror wandered off-screen during a break and didn't hear the people on the screen calling him back.

Still, much of the new technology has been lauded as a positive thing, and even after the pandemic, much of it will likely remain in use for reasons of transparency and flexibility. Michigan Chief Justice Bridget Mary McCormack said of the impact, "The pandemic was not the disruption we wanted, but the disruption we needed."

and experience of a court reporter with the speed and power of computers," writes Teshima.

New technologies in the workplace often require a period of adjustment. Older courthouses might require extensive rewiring. Circuits need to be able to accommodate multiple devices running at once. There needs to be a secure high-speed Internet system in place. Lawyers need to be able to connect their laptops to the Internet as well as the computer equipment in the courthouse. Some judges and attorneys might not be comfortable with all the new "gadgets."

The social distancing required by the pandemic meant that courthouse IT departments had to install new equipment and train people to use it very quickly. Rather than something used only occasionally, webcams and screens are now the way a great deal of the court's daily business is being conducted.

CHAPTER 6

GETTING STARTED

Deciding on a career as a lawyer is a big decision. Law school is a very serious investment in time and money. The first prerequisite is a four-year college degree. There's no particular pre-law curriculum. The American Bar Association recommends a challenging program to prepare you for the rigors of law school.

Business, history, or political science might seem like obvious choices, but even science or the arts can be a good foundation, as lawyers deal with all facets of society. The goal is to prepare yourself for a career that will involve a great deal of reading, research, and critical thinking. If the idea of spending hours at the library doesn't

All lawyers spend a great deal of time reading and doing research. This is something you should consider carefully when making your career choice.

appeal to you, you might consider a different field of criminal justice.

Lawyers also need to have good computer skills. While much research is done using books, some is done online. Criminal lawyers need to know how to connect their laptops and operate the technology used to present evidence in the courtroom. Attorneys of all types will find themselves increasingly dependent on video conferencing.

Many undergraduate schools have pre-law advisers who give students guidance on what core skills they need to develop. Most commonly, these skills include:

- Analytic/problem-solving skills
- Critical reading
- Writing skills, especially persuasive writing
- Oral communication/listening abilities
- General research skills with computers, books, and interviews
- Task organization/management skills
- Public service and promotion of justice
- Vocabulary acquisition
- Familiarity with libraries and resources

In addition, experts recommend students develop:

- Wide understanding of U.S. history, including how society, politics, economics, and the culture have affected it
- Fundamental comprehension of political thought and the U.S. political system

- Basic awareness of math and financial skills
- Concepts related to human behavior and social interaction
- Familiarity with diverse cultures within and beyond the United States, as well as knowledge of world events and the interdependence of this nation with others

GETTING A TASTE OF THE REAL THING

Reading career guides and biographies is a terrific way to start thinking about a career in law. However, seven years of college is a huge commitment, and you should try to get some first-hand experience before you start looking at schools. If your high school offers mock trial or debate as activities, these are a good chance to try out some of the skills that lawyers use. They also look good on your transcript.

Do you enjoy the research that goes into building a successful argument? Are you confident speaking in front of people? Are you comfortable with the idea of a career that requires conservative dress and appearance in the workplace?

If your answer is "yes," you should look into a summer legal program designed for teens. Some programs are very elaborate—and expensive. They might last a week or more and include living in the dorms at a law school. This gives students a taste of what attending law school will be like. This can be a valuable experience, but it's not something every

Learning to speak in a courtroom takes practice. It's not just about public speaking but also about following the protocols of the courtroom.

family can afford. There are merit-based programs that are free or offer scholarships. Your guidance counselor can help you find something that works for you and your budget.

PAYING FOR LAW SCHOOL

Most people will agree that lawyers earn a comfortable living. However, to land that well-paying job, you first have to get your degree and that can be expensive. Tuition at some schools can be $50,000 per year—and tuition isn't the only cost. You'll also need textbooks and a laptop, room and board if you choose a school away from home, plus other expenses. The financial aid office of the school you're interested in can give you a clear idea of what your degree will cost at that particular institution.

There are many factors to consider when deciding how to finance your law degree. You don't have to attend an Ivy League school. There may be an accredited law school at a local university. You could also attend a community college, which costs far less than other colleges, as a jumping-off point. You should investigate grants, scholarships or work/study programs you might be eligible for. Student loans need to be repaid after graduation, and you need to consider how that will impact your budget when you're first starting out in your law career. There are loan forgiveness programs for graduates who choose a career in public service. Some are federal and others vary by state.

You can also check the website for your local courthouse to see if they have any tours or programs for students. Finding a free or low-cost summer program can take a lot more research than finding an expensive one. However, if you're interested in a career that's all about solving problems with logic and research, consider that your first challenge.

Myths and Facts About Working in the Court System

Myth: All U.S. Supreme Court justices have been lawyers or judges.
Fact: Prior to 1941, there were justices who studied law informally (with a local judge or lawyer), attended law school but didn't graduate, and even one who never attended law school at all.

Myth: Convicted felons can't become lawyers.
Fact: Not necessarily. A few states do bar convicted felons from practicing law. Others allow it if the person is able to successfully argue to the licensing authority that they are a person of good moral character.

Myth: Supreme Court Justices serve for life.
Fact: Many do, but they may also choose to retire, or be removed by impeachment.

The legal profession is expected to need a good deal more employees in the coming years. This could make it a very good field in which to prepare for a job.

With so many jobs to pursue in the field of law, there's a lot for young people to consider. Not everyone becomes a judge or lawyer. What type of job would you like in the field of law?

Myth: The U.S. Constitution gives justices final say on laws.
Fact: Nothing in the Constitution gives the Supreme Court that power. In the late 1800s, however, Congress gave the Supreme Court the right to review any federal case. Not long after, the justices gained the right to refuse any case as well.

Myth: All attorneys are rich.
Fact: The attorneys who make the most are employed by the largest firms, but that's only about 1 percent of the world's law firms. Most work in smaller firms. The money tends to be good, but it's not as much as many think—especially with the massive amount of student debt attorneys tend to have.

Myth: Most of the work that trial attorneys do is inside the courtroom.
Fact: Only a very small amount of civil cases ever go to trial. Most are settled out of court or in other ways. Most work in the legal field isn't glamorous—in fact, it's often mostly writing and research.

Myth: Lawyers have to be good at arguing.
Fact: Sometimes this is true. However, most lawyers need to be able to work with other people and reach an agreement. Persuasion and research are often more helpful than arguing.

GLOSSARY

bailiff: Court official charged with securing the courtroom.

battery: The crime of battering or beating someone.

captioning: Converting the spoken word to written word or translating.

cross-examine: To ask questions of a witness in order to check or discredit his or her previous testimony.

deposition: A witness's testimony.

dissenter: In a legal sense, one who disagrees with a majority decision.

forensics: Application of science to legal problems.

idioms: Expressions in the usage of language that have a peculiar or nonstandard meaning.

impartial: Fair, unbiased, or without prejudice.

jurisdiction: The limits or territory within which a person or group can exercise authority.

legal secretary: Person who does clerical duties in a law firm or private practice.

litigant: Person or party involved in a lawsuit.

paralegal: Lawyer's assistant.

pro bono: Describing legal work done for no cost.

proficiency: Thorough skillfulness.

prosecuting attorney: Lawyer charged with showing why a defendant is guilty.

quarantine: To force into isolation.

sequester: To isolate or set apart from others.

stenomask: Handheld recording mask used by court reporters.

stenotype: Recording instrument used by court reporters.

tactile signing: Sign language for those who are both visually and hearing impaired.

testimony: Evidence given in court.

torts: Legal classification of wrongful acts.

verdict: Official court judgment.

vocational: Relating to a job or career skills.

FOR MORE INFORMATION

American Bar Association (ABA)
321 N. Clark Street
Chicago, IL 60654
(800) 285-2221
Website: www.americanbar.org
The ABA is the professional organization for those who practice law in the United States. It provides accreditation for law schools and sets the standards for professional conduct in the legal industry.

Canadian Bar Association (CBA)
66 Slater St., Ste. 1200
Ottawa, ON K1P 5H1
(613) 237-2925
Website: cba.org
The Canadian Bar Association (CBA) is the professional organization for those who practice law in Canada.

Law School Admission Council (LSAC)
662 Penn St.
Newtown, PA 18940
(215) 968-1001
Website: lsac.org
The LSAC administers the Law School Admission Test (LSAT) and provides information for students interested in a law career.

National Association of Legal Assistants (NALA)
7666 E. 61st St., Ste. 315
Tulsa, OK 74133
(918) 587-6828
Website: www.nala.org
The NALA is the professional organization for paralegals.

National Association for Legal Professionals (NALS)
3502 Woodview Trace, Ste. 300
Indianapolis, IN 46268
(918) 582-5188
Website: www.nals.org
The NALS offers educational and professional advice and support for those interested in careers in the legal services industry.

National High School Mock Trial Championship (NHSMTC)
Website: nationalmocktrial.org
The NHSMTC promotes interest in the legal profession through student participation in mock trials and other academic activities.

FOR FURTHER READING

Baum, Lawrence. *The Supreme Court 13th Edition*. Washington, D.C.: Congressional Quarterly Press, 2018.

Carmon, Irin. *Notorious RBG Young Reader's Edition: The Life and Times of Ruth Bader Ginsburg*. New York, NY: Harper Collins, 2017.

Friedman, Jane M. *America's First Woman Lawyer: The Biography of Myra Bradwell.* Amherst, NY: Prometheus Books, (Reprint edition) 2019.

Grant, Heath, and Karen Terry. *Law Enforcement in the 21st Century 4th Edition*. Carmel, IN: Pearson, 2016.

Hatch, Scott A., and Lisa Hatch. *Paralegal Career for Dummies*. Hoboken, NJ: John Wiley and Sons, Inc., 2019.

National Learning Corporation. *Legal Secretary (1343) (Career Examination Series)*. Syosset, NY: Passbooks, 2019.

Reeves, Diane Lindsey. *Career Ideas for Teens in Law and Public Safety*. New York, NY: Checkmark Books, 2006.

Schroeder, Donald, and Frank A. Lombardo. *Court Officer Exam (Barron's Test Prep) 4th Edition*. Hauppauge, NY: Barron's Educational Series, 2019.

Weatherford, Carole Boston. *Great African American Lawyers: Raising the Bar of Freedom.* Berkeley Heights, NJ: Enslow Publishers, 2003.

Wick, Kenneth A. *The Essential 99 Punctuation Rules for Court Reporters: Student Edition.* Independently published, 2019.

INDEX

A

B

C

ABOUT THE AUTHOR

Kathleen A. Klatte is the author of several nonfiction books for children and teens. Topics range from animals to constitutional law to even more animals. She also works as a costumer for historic sites and local theaters. Her credits include the short films *Runaway* and *The Misadventures of Ichabod Crane*, and the online documentary *People Not Property*, all for Historic Hudson Valley. Kathleen lives in New York with one cat and far too many books and Legos.

CREDITS

Cover (main image) DarrenMower/E+/Getty Images; (background texture) SRM Company/Shutterstock.com; p. 5 New York Daily News Archive/Getty Images; p. 9 trekandshoot/iStock/Getty Images; p. 11 Spiderplay/iStock/Getty Images; p. 12 Pool/Getty Images; p. 16 Jose Perez/Bauer-Griffin/GC Images/Getty Images; pp. 18, 41 Bob Riha Jr./Archive Photos/Getty Images; p. 22 Daniel Grill/Getty Images; p. 23 https://commons.wikimedia.org/wiki/Category:Stenographs_(typewriters)#/media/File:PrimerStenoMashinki.svg; p. 25 Mark Wilson/Getty Images; p. 27 Fuse/Corbis/Getty Images; p. 30 moodboard/Getty Images; p. 32 rubberball/Getty Images; p. 34 Pool Photographer/WireImage/Getty Images; p. 37 https://en.wikipedia.org/wiki/File:Mary-Margaret-Bartelme-Bain.jpeg; p. 39 Corbis Historical/Getty Images; p. 43 https://commons.wikimedia.org/wiki/File:Ruth_Bader_Ginsburg_2016_portrait.jpg; p. 45 Maskot/Getty Images; p. 49 Heide Benser/The Image Bank/Getty Images; p. 51 Junial Enterprises/Shutterstock.com; p. 57 Bloomberg/Getty Images; p. 59 Chris Ryan/OJO Images/Getty Images; p. 61 Helen King/Corbis/Getty Images; p. 64 Archive Photos/Stringer/Getty Images; p. 66 MediaNews Group/Bay Area News/Getty Images; p. 68 wavebreakmedia/Shutterstock.com; p. 71 ruthrose/E+/Getty Images; p. 73 Ja Crispy/Shutterstock.com; p. 75 picture alliance/Getty Images; p. 78 https://en.wikipedia.org/wiki/File:Supreme_court_preview_2007.JPG; p. 81 Ronny Hartmann/AFP/Getty Images; p. 85 Tashi-Delek/E+/Getty Images; p. 88 Igor Alecsander/E+/Getty Images; p. 91 Guy Cali/The Image Bank/Getty Images; p. 92 everything possible/Shutterstock.com.

Designer: Michael Flynn; Editor: Greg Roza